1

Real Estate for Beginners:

The complete guide for those who want to start a career in the real estate sector

Carniel Moorblade

PUBLISHED BY:

Carniel Moorblade

Copyright © 2021

The content within this book has been derived from various sources. Please consult a licensed professional before attempting any techniques outlined in this book.

By reading this document, the reader agrees that under no circumstances is the author responsible for any losses, direct or indirect, which are incurred as a result of the use of information contained within this document, including, but not limited to, — errors, omissions, or inaccuracies.

Table of Contents

About Carniel

Carniel Moorblade, Attorney at Law, is licensed to practice law in Texas, North Carolina, Virginia and the District of Columbia. He has a B.B.A. in Finance from the University of Houston School of Business, and he has a Juris Doctor (J.D.) in Law from the University of Texas School of Law. He is admitted to practice in all Courts in Texas, North Carolina, Virginia, and the District of Columbia, as well as the U.S. Tax Court, U.S. Federal District Court, Eastern District of Texas, and the D.C. Court of Appeals. He practices in the fields of Tax Law, Real Estate Law, Corporate and Business Law, and Wills, Trusts and Estates. He is a member of The National Society of Accountants. Formerly a Tax Examiner for the IRS, and a Tax Accountant for a Big 8 Accounting Firm, he has also been a Newspaper Reporter, Radio Announcer, Radio News Director, Television Reporter and Anchorman, Television Executive News Producer, and Military Intelligence Analyst. As an elected County Attorney, responsible for Criminal Misdemeanor Prosecution, he handled over 2,000 cases. In addition to 40 years practicing law, he built one of the first computerized Abstract Plants, and operated his own Title Insurance Company, becoming an Approved Title Attorney for seven national Title Insurance Underwriters. He has handled over 2,000 real estate closings. Prior to his law career, he was a Radio Announcer at WQTE in Detroit during the "Motown" era, and he was a DJ at KIKK in Houston when it was named "Country Music Station of the Year" by Billboard Magazine. He collects and refurbishes Vintage Audio Equipment. He has written and produced more than 1,000 half-hour Television Newscasts.

He has written over 700 stories as a Newspaper Reporter.
He has logged over 8,000 hours on the radio.
He is a Lifetime Member of Mensa.
As a Real Estate Investor, his activities have ranged from travel trailers to office buildings, and from on-campus condos to rural land.
He was named a Top Writer by Quora.com where his Answers have been viewed more than 1,930,000 times.

Introduction

With the concept of real estate, the first thing that comes to people's minds is selling and buying houses.

Some think that you need to have excellent communication and marketing skills in order to succeed in your career if you're into real estate. They say that it's all about the talk, the eye contact, and the perfect sales pitches to say. But then again, there's more to real estate than selling houses and good sales talk.

Real estate is very a stable business to be part of. One of the basic needs in life is shelter; a habitat that can keep you safe and protected from whatever dangers and weather out there. A house is more than a structure. It's a place to call home; a sanctuary.

On the business of real estate, it is actually land and anything that is attached to it - with value. It deals with anything and everything that has to do with property and land ownership. And always remember: location is everything. It really is all about the location.

In terms of money, real estate can be very lucrative. Learn all the terminology and the basic fundamentals, and not only will you be able to survive long enough to know the ropes - you'll thrive. Along the way, familiarize yourself with a list of common real estate terms and their meanings. By then, you are ready for the actual business of real estate.

Chapter 1: What is Real Estate?

Real estate consists of the land and anything that is attached to it. It includes immovable attachments to it: buildings, fixtures, appurtenances, fences, roadways, renovations, improvements, plants, structures, sewers and utility systems. Simply put, it is the land and everything on it. It may also be called real property.

There are different types of real estate out there but it can be divided into two kinds: income generating and non-income generating. The types of real estate that are income generating are Office property, Retail property, Industrial property and Multi-family residential property. The types of real estate that are non-income generating are personal homes, vacation properties and vacant commercial buildings.

Office Property

For certain real property, owner's office properties are termed as a "flagship investment". This is the case because office properties are often very high profile and are often the physically largest properties. Image from Flicker by Hamson.

The typical location of this type of property is almost always at the core of downtown areas. The return on investment on office properties can highly vary, depending on the overall economic performance where such property is located.

A downside of this type of property is that it has very high costs for its operations. For instance, let's say you own an office property. If you lose your tenants, it can drastically affect the return-on-investment for your property.

Otherwise, in times when your property - as well as its location - is in demand and you have multiple tenants, these properties tend to perform extremely well. This is due to the fact that rental rates skyrocket once demand for a certain property increases. The demand for such property is directly affected by the what each prospective or current tenant company requires - with regards to the office space they can provide their workers.

Usually, office workers are engaged in activities and tasks like accounting, insurance, management, and administration. It has been observed that as the number of these "white collar jobs" increase, the demand for office space also increases.

Another factor that can greatly affect investing in an office property would be the time it takes for you to build the office space that possible tenants would want to rent. This may include building the walls and rooms needed for space, to building the complex itself.

Retail Property

There are many different types of this kind of property, since it may range from single tenant buildings to large enclosed shopping malls. When it comes to this property, an anchor is pretty much a staple. Image from Flicker by Juris

An anchor is a very large and a well-known retailer that draws people to the property. An illustration would be Wal-Mart; it is an anchor of a lot of retail properties. If the property has a food store as its anchor, it is said to be food anchored. On the other hand, if the property has a grocery store as an anchor it is said to be grocery-anchored. These anchors are important since these make the property more desirable for investing in. Retail properties also have commercial retail units. These units are called ancillary multi-bay buildings, which have smaller tenants in them.

The demand for this type of property can be affected by a lot of different factors. The factors that may affect the demand for this property are: location, population density, visibility, relative income levels and population growth. This property is said to perform well when the economy is growing and the growth in retail sales is high.

In terms of investing for real estate, this type of property is more preferred compared to Office property. This is because the return on investment for retail property is more stable than the return on investing for office property. It is said to be more stable since retail leases are longer and retailers do not usually relocate often as compared to office tenants.

9

This type of property is often in the portfolio of an average real estate investor since it requires a smaller investment and has lower operating costs than the office property and retail property. Industrial properties have different types and these types depend on what they are used for. Image from Flicker by Judith Hanlock

For instance, this property can be used for warehousing, research and development, manufacturing, or even for distribution purposes. W when it comes to this type of property, the relevant factors would be: its location relative to major routes, the functionality of the space, and building configuration. Certain situations require a covered yard, although some instances do not.

Multi-family Residential Property

This type of property has the most stable return. Why? Because no matter how bad or how good the economy is, people always need a place to live. When it comes to this type of property, the loss of a tenant has a negligible effect on the investor's return or the bottom line. Almost always, another tenant will just come along. Image from Flicker by Gerry

For real estate to be considered multi-family residential property, it has to be a building with at least two housing units - residential dwellings with bedrooms, bathrooms, kitchen, and all other housing necessities. On the small scale, it can be a two-flat building with a basement suite and upper floors; on the large scale, it can be an entire apartment building.

Purchasing a single-family unit is great but the returns you get will likely not be enough to sustain you. However, you can choose to invest in multifamily properties. These properties contain two, three, or four units. The advantage of choosing this option is that you can secure one loan and you can comfortably live off the returns without the need for another source of income.

Single-family homes

Many investors find it easier to invest in single-family homes. This is because the process is relatively simple and you only have to deal with one tenant at a time. Thus, it is easier to manage the property. It is also easier to come up with the money to purchase a single-family unit. Image from Flicker by Dennis

Mobile homes

Purchasing and renting out mobile homes may be the way to go if you have some little cash as they cost relatively less than other housing units do. You may decide to put a mobile home on its own land or use a mobile park. Image from Flicker Berth

Small apartments

Investing in a small apartment building can lead to significant cash flow. The building can have five to fifty units. You can also use a live-in manager to make your work easier. The manager can be responsible for things like dealing with tenants and performing maintenance and repairs. You can pay the manager by allowing him or her to live in a unit for free or by greatly reducing the amount of rent your manager pays. Image from Flicker by Jenny

Large apartments

Another option you can invest in is large apartments. These are apartments with more than fifty units. A full time staff often runs such apartments. They also have amenities such as swimming pools, garages, and workout areas. Often, individuals come together to purchase large apartment units. Image from Flicker by Oliver

Commercial property

Commercial real estate investing is big business. Unfortunately, it is usually a preserve of those who have a lot of money to spend. This is because commercial property may often experience periods of vacancies especially during tough economic times. This is because returns depend on businesses flourishing and if they don't, the businesses end up vacating the premises and it may take a while to find a new tenant. Image from Flicker by Marissa

It is important that you think carefully about the niche or option you want to invest in. Later, as you become an expert, you can delve into other options.

Chapter 2: Making Money with Real Estate

There are a lot of ways to make money with real estate, although all these ways can be summed up to three concepts. These concepts are:

1. When the value of the property has significantly increased compared to its purchase price or its previous value

2. Rentals that could be collected by leasing out the property to prospective tenants

3. Business activities which depend on the real estate that generates profit

These are the three ways in which almost all of the real estate investors make money.

How to Settle for An Option

Once you decide to engage in real estate investing, you need to select a niche (option) to concentrate on. As a beginner, whatever knowledge you have is second hand knowledge. This means that although you may have read a lot or spoken to experts in the field, you are yet to face real life situations. Focusing on one option will enable you to learn a lot and gain the needed experience. Settling for an option depends on several things. These are:

Cash

Your real estate investing option will largely depend on the amount of cash you can raise or you can borrow. For example, if you want to concentrate on commercial property, you may need to raise millions of dollars.

Property tax

Property tax tends to differ across the board. This means you have to carefully calculate how much you will be paying in taxes and add that amount to the rest of your expenses to determine your cash flow. If you notice the amount remaining is too little, you may want to look into another niche. Image from Kali

Insurance

You cannot forego insurance when you invest in real estate: the bigger your investment the larger your insurance payments. Keep this in mind when

Neighborhood

The neighborhood also plays a role in which option you choose. For example, you may want to develop high-end apartments in a poor neighborhood or a crime-filled neighborhood. If you do this, chances are, you will have a problem getting tenants, as your target market will not be in the area. So, take your time to choose carefully the kind of neighborhood you want to purchase your property.

Future development

You also need to discover what future developments are planned for in the area you want to purchase real estate. These developments may work to your advantage or disadvantage. For example, if there is a plan to build a park, you can attract many families as renters. However, if another investor who has more cash than you plan to build a series of apartments and offers them at a cheaper rent than you, then you might be in trouble.

Amenities

Amenities are important especially if you want to invest in family units. Check promotional literature to see what type of amenities are available in a particular city. This will come in handy when you

are marketing your property. Image from Flicker by Gerry

Schools

Families or younger couples who may eventually start their own families will be interested in the type of schools near your property. You may have a great property targeting families but you may lose out on tenants because the area lacks good schools or the area is near a college hence filled with college going students. Check out the area before deciding on what to invest in. Image from Flicker by Maey

Crime

Crime is bad for everyone especially for those who are running businesses. No business owner would want to get an office space in a place known for crime even if the said space is big and cheap. You can find out the crime rate of an area by visiting the police or a public library before you can decide to purchase property in a particular niche.

Involvement

You must decide to what extent you want to be involved in managing the property. For example, if you invest in a single-family unit, you may rarely need to be involved in the unit. However, if you invest in apartment buildings, you may need to stay there fully or hire a live-in manager.

Knowledge is crucial when it comes to real estate investing. Learn, listen, observe and use your instincts as you find your footing and become an expert in the real estate investing field. Now that you have probably selected the niche that you want to invest in, the next step is to know how to make money in the particular niche you have chosen.

Increase in property value?

Unfortunately, the value of properties does not always increase. This can be seen during the past few years. Worst case scenario, these values cannot even beat inflation.

For instance, you purchase a piece of property worth $500,000. You may be able to sell the property for $515,000 after a year when the inflation rate is at 3%, but you will notice that that $15,000 profit does not affect your purchasing power. Why? Its value is the same as when you purchased it. Now how is that so? The profit you received was not real; it was merely enough to cover the inflation rate during that year. Hence, you are not actually $15,000 richer than you were the year before. This kind of situation likely arises when the government has to make money, but it spends more than it has collected in taxes.

You must be asking then, "How then do investors make money with their real estate holdings?"

These investors make money when they take advantage of certain situations.

One is when the inflation rate is predicted to exceed the current rate of long-term debt - in other words, the national prime interest rate. When this happens, you will notice that there are people purchasing properties and they are even willing to take out a loan to purchase those properties. These people are willing to take the risk.

This is because they are paying off the mortgage of those purchased properties with dollars' worth less than their value. At first, this shows a saver becoming a debtor. In fact, a lot of investors made money this way in the 1970s and the early 1980s when the inflation was spiraling out of control.

Another is when the overall cost of real estate, including property prices rental/lease rates, is projected to rise due to overall demand within a certain location. An example would be an increasingly live able city. If the overall demand for residential and commercial property rises faster than the amount of real estate available, prices rise. Intelligent investors would acquire property beforehand, then sit back and enjoy the gains.

Rental Income

Making money from renting out property is a very lucrative source of income.

A great illustration of that would be a game of monopoly. If you have interest in a house, an apartment building, a hotel or an office building, then you can rent those out and collect rent in exchange for letting them utilize those buildings.

A useful tool in making money from these properties is the capitalization rate. This rate is a special financial ratio: the value for the property on sale is divided by the value they earn per year. For instance, your apartment building may be sold for a million dollars, yet it earns one hundred thousand dollars a year in rental income. One million dollars is divided by the hundred thousand dollars - which gives us a ratio of 10 percent. Thus, you can expect a 10 percent return on your investment if you purchased the said property in cash and without any debt in acquiring it.

If you still want to use debt to acquire that property, it's still quite advantageous. As long as the rental income exceeds the monthly mortgage or loan cost, cash and equity still go into your pocket.

Business Operations

This type of operation involves business activities and special services. For instance, you are the owner of an office building and you may generate income through vending machines placed in the building and for pay parking. You are able to earn income not just by renting your property out, but by providing income-generating goods and services. In addition, you can also rent out your property, or have a business that you operate.

Cash flow

Once you buy your property, you should set about getting tenants who will afford the rent that will make you gain profit. Your cash flow, the cash you get after paying for all your expenses, will depend on the rent you set. You should set a rent amount that will allow you to take care of your expenses and still make a profit.

Supplementary income

When you invest in real estate, you should stay alert to other income making opportunities that come with your investment. You can make money from:

*Vending machines

*Laundry facilities

*Storage units

*Car washes

Observe what other property owners are offering and listen to the needs of your tenants. For example, if a tenant complains about a lack of a certain service, see how you can incorporate that service and turn it into profit.

Appreciation

The real estate market changes mostly for the better; the trick is to know when to take advantage of the changes. For example, if an amenity is built near your property, you can take advantage of this in your advertising or selling.

Many investors who invest in real estate make their purchases when there is a slump and sell when prices are high. Also, you can revamp your property to make it attractive to both buyers and renters and thus fetch more.

Related income

As you get better in real estate investing, you will realize that you can do some things to increase your income. For example, you can become a paid consultant or you can take on managing responsibilities for those who own properties but don't want to get involved in managing. Many individuals manage property in order to get a percentage of the rent.

Clearly, you need to think beyond the obvious if you want to make real estate investing your business. When you see a piece of real estate, don't just think of rent money as the way to get cash. However, in order to start making money, you need to have a plan.

Chapter 3: Important things to know

A good buyer is a good researcher. Ultimately, the more information a buyer has, the more power he/she wields.

However, not all information available out there is relevant to a prospective purchase. That is why you must know what information is important.

Here are some things that would help a prospective buyer:

1. You must learn the lay of the land

This can be done by simply driving around the area of the property you would want to acquire. You must never assume that you already know the area simply because you have purchased others like it before.

You must observe the access routes in the area, its accessibility to public transportation, the nearby stores and the nearby school district. It would be helpful if you would also look at the neighborhood and determine whether it is a suitable place for your prospective buyers in the future.

Here is another hidden trick you need to know. Make additional observations LATE NIGHT at both a weekend and a weekday. Why? Because the area around the property may have a different face at night. There may be a few too many loitering people that may seem troublesome. There may be street prostitutes, gangs, or drug dealers hanging around. There may be one too many police/ambulance sirens. There may not be enough streetlights. Anything.

And if the area doesn't pose TOO much of a threat at night, then it may be safe to acquire after all.

2. You must make some on-the-ground research

This is the time for you to get out of your car and talk to locals. You should consider going to the areas where locals love to go to, then ask them about the area. It would be helpful to get the opinion of your friends or your family that reside nearby. You should also try going to the town hall so that you can see if there are developments to be done in the near future. This way, you can also understand how the town works since you can ask for plans of the town. Thus, with all the information you have gathered, you can now predict who your future buyers would be and you can now know what to do to your prospective property to make it more attractive once you purchase it.

3. You must make a sales comparison

It is necessary that you compare prices of properties that are similar to the one you would like to buy. This is done so you know how much you are going to invest - and if it is worth the money you are going to pay it with.

4. You must educate yourself with market rents

Since rent is a staple when it comes to real estate, knowing how much you are expecting to earn would be very helpful. You would then be able to determine the cash inflow you can set aside for reserves and for contingencies. This way, you can tell whether such property is a good source of rental income - or not. Then, you could assess whether you should invest more into rehabilitating it or not buying it at all.

5. You must check with the local registry of deeds

This part is very important, since now you are checking if the property you are about to buy has any encumbrances attached to it - or if you are going to have absolute title over it. It is preferred that you purchase a property with no encumbrances at all so that you would be able to exercise all right of ownership over it and you could avoid a lot of problems that arise when the property is encumbered.

6. You must make a list of all possible costs

You must list down all costs that you think are to be incurred. These costs may include taxes, repairs and maintenance costs, insurance fees, and utilities expense. It is better that you project a higher probable cost than incur costs that are way beyond what you expected to spend so that you are better prepared.

7. You must make a comparison of multiple properties

You must a have a short list of all the properties you would want to purchase. Then, you should make a pros and cons list for each property.

This way, you are able to select the best property out of the bunch. Sometimes, including a property you do not like at all can be helpful if it can provide you some insights as to what kind of property you are looking for.

8. You must obtain local statistics

Getting this data enables you to see how that area is doing compared to other areas. You can also see if the people in the local area are all employed - thus they can be viable buyers. Or, if the unemployment rate in the area is increasing.

You can also determine if the population is growing or if it has reached its limit. You can also see if the real estate taxes in a certain area would be much more practical than the others you have seen. All this data will help you in determining if the property really is as attractive as it seems - or if your realtor was just a good salesman.

9. You must determine the potential of each property

The end goal here is to eventually sell, rent out, or lease the property for a profit. Before that can be done, you need to know the good and bad information about that property so that you can likely create a better profit.

You need to know what you can and cannot do with the property. The flexibility of a certain property is an important factor. If you are able to use it for a number of causes, that makes the property way more attractive and this would certainly attract buyers.

10. You must study the data on permits needed

You must know what permits you are going to obtain and the costs that come with those permits. This is so that you can gauge how much you are going to spend on them and how long it will take you to acquire all the permits necessary for a property.

Chapter 4: First-Time Investor Mistakes

For first-time investors, it is quite normal to make mistakes. But it is unforgivable to make these mistakes when they could have been avoided with the right information the investor should have known with a little research.

Here are some of the mistakes that are most-commonly committed by real estate investors:

1. Adapting a stock market mentality

2. Making a blind investment

3. Having no cash reserves

4. Being too focused on the cash

5. Not treating it like a business

1. Adapting a stock market mentality

Did you know that ninety percent of new investors think that they would make a killing in the real estate market because they knew someone who did, often due to the fast appreciation of their property value in the past? What these people do not quite understand is that buying real estate properties for its appreciation during a short period of time is very risky. Often, you are not certain whether the property will indeed appreciate during the time period you expect it to.

Real estate investments are mostly held for long-term profits. It would be wise for you to keep a cash reserve. So, when the market goes bad and you are expected to take losses by selling away certain properties, the loss would be lessened by your reserve without you going totally broke.

2. Making a blind investment

As a matter of fact, real estate is one of the very few investments where risk is very much proportional to the knowledge of the buyer. It would be best for a future buyer to learn about investing techniques, acquisition and negotiation, financing and the local marketplace. This is important; done right, he/she will be able to determine if the real property he/she is about to purchase is worth the money spent. Knowledge makes your investment less risky, thus making it a safer investment.

3. Having no cash reserves

The most important term that you should keep in mind when you invest in real estate is cash flow. Hands down.

You must have cash reserves so that you can stay in the real estate business for a long time. Purchasing a piece of real estate is quite easy, but how are you going to handle it if that property does not generate the expected income and you have to spend money to repair it, on top of the other expenses that keep cropping up? The answer to that question is cash reserves. If you are able to weather through the toughest situations, then you will always come out on top when it comes to this business.

For instance, you have no cash reserves and you purchase an apartment building that is a fixer-upper. You spend on repairs and you are pressured into accepting unqualified tenants just for the sake that money would come in. You even give in to the unreasonable demands your tenant is demanding. It is quite a terrible situation, right? But if you have cash reserves, then you can actually hold out for a tenant who is willing to pay you the right rent, you can hold on to the property until the right price is offered to you, and you can easily fix up the building without suffering losses.

You can buy properties without the necessary cash on hand but you cannot survive the real estate game without any cash in reserve. You must consider earning the necessary reserves before buying any property.

4. Being too focused on the cash

Being greedy can ruin great deals for you. Buying and selling properties at a profit is a good deal, but waiting for that perfect deal and losing a good one is nonsense.

You must know when you are being dealt a good hand. And that is signified by a profit - no matter how small it may be. If the deal is profitable, then take it and move on to the next property. This way, you have generated cash reserves and made a profit as well. Yet, you must learn to know when enough is enough.

5. Not treating it like a business

Real estate is business. It takes time for the property to appreciate, to learn how and what properties to buy and to create relationships with buyers. Investing your money is not the only thing you must do; you must invest the necessary time and energy too. You must set your expectations to a reasonable standard and you must take the necessary action for you to be able to fully utilize the properties you have.

Chapter 5: "Location, Location, Location..."

"You are not a tree, you can move" – Jimmy Napier

When entering the business of real estate location is a primary consideration and a lot of effort goes into researching the following:

1. The area of the country where the property is located

2. The city in which it is located

3. Whether the property is in a subdivision or not

4. The value of the homes in the same area

5. Do you need to hire someone to rehabilitate the property?

6. You need to find the right tenant to lease it out

7. When you need to sell the property

For you to be able to make your investment a safe one, you may reduce certain risks by considering some factors before purchasing a property.

There are things that you must avoid when it comes to certain properties:

1. You must avoid areas near the water, due to the high cost of insuring such property. There are exceptions to this, particularly if the overall potential income of such property is too tempting to pass.

2. You must calculate the taxes that are to be paid for such property, since some states have very high taxes when it comes to properties.

4. You must consider the climate in the area as well, since the climate can affect certain structures.

5. You must buy a property in a place where people want to live in. It is a place where the area is quite beautiful, lively, and welcoming. Consider how short the distance is between the property and certain points of interest, including shopping malls, supermarkets, restaurants, and even the downtown core.

6. It's best if there is a nearby school district too - it certainly increases the property value of the nearby properties.

7. You would want to purchase a property where people would most likely immigrate to.

Chapter 6: The Return on Investment

Cash Flow is Everything!

After you purchase the property, the hard work begins. Now that an outflow of cash has occurred, or that a huge debt has been incurred, you must think of ways to make an inflow of cash.

It would be best if there would be a constant cash inflow after you have purchased the property. There are ways where you can make such inflow. For instance, you have purchased a house and it's quite a good find. It is even fit for living in. Now you can start leasing it out to qualified tenants. You can keep leasing it out until you earn the necessary cash reserve to either remodel that house or build a new one or you can keep leasing it out.

If you have a constant inflow of cash, then you can have the necessary cash reserves to protect yourself from losses in the market - or for necessary repairs required for property maintenance. Cash flow not just gives you the cash reserves you need, but it also gives you profit.

1. Cash inflow from rent

A property can provide a steady source of income in the form of rental payments. This way, it is like a stock that pays dividends. Although, the owner of the property has more control over the rent he/she receives - as compared to a stockholder and the dividends given.

2. Appreciation

Through the years, it has been proven that real estate properties are a good source of income once the value of the property increases over time. But the appreciation in property values is tricky to predict since there are a number of variables that can affect it.

3. Improvements on property

Your property can be improved so that when it is time to liquidate it, you can have a better deal on the table. These improvements can be done while the property is being rented out and over a period of time too. You can hold on to your property until you are satisfied with all the improvements that need to be done and until you are able to obtain the best deal for it.

4. Inflation

Did you know that inflation is your friend and not your enemy? Inflation increases construction costs but it also increases rent. This is a good for you, since you can hike up those rentals as the inflation rate increases. Another factor that can drive up the rent is population growth - which in turn creates housing demands.

5. Settling your mortgage

As you are slowly paying off your debt, your equity is slowly increasing as well. These increases can be utilized for other purposes, such as making other investments in real estate or other profitable ventures. Image from Flicker by Larry

Chapter 7: Real Estate Terms to Know

Next, you have a list of terms that'll come in handy once the time comes. You may not have to read all of them at once, but refer to them often - especially when you're analyzing your next real estate deal or plan.

Mortgage Terminology

Almost always, you'll have to set up a mortgage to finance your next property (unless you have a good amount of cash to spare).

Fortunately, there are many different mortgage types out there.

Read through the chapter and, for your next Real Estate investment, select the best mortgage suited for your real estate investing goals. Ideally, you want to choose the one which gives you the best possible cash flow, given all other factors.

100% Mortgage

This is a mortgage loan wherein the borrower is given a loan amount which is equal to the total value of the property bought by that same borrower.

During these instances, the borrower is not required to provide a down payment for such loan. This type of loan gives a person, who has little or no monetary resource, the opportunity to buy a house or some other real estate property.

Usually, this loan is secured by stocks and bonds which are owned by the person borrowing.

The negative side when it comes to these loans is that they come with much higher interest rates and the securities which are used as security would probably be liquidated to cover the debts owed by borrower.

125% Loan

It is a loan with an initial amount which is equal to a hundred and twenty-five percent of the initial value of the property which has been purchased. This type of loan is very risky since it carries with it a very high interest rate.

2-1 Buydown

It is a certain type of mortgage wherein there is a set of two interest rates: initial and temporary. Then, the interest begins to increase in a stair-step fashion until such time that a permanent interest rate is set. The temporary interest rates are reduced by the borrower paying for it or by a builder as an incentive in purchasing a home.

During certain instances, the cost of the buydown is computed and then placed in an account of escrow. Then monthly payments are made which are equivalent to the difference in the temporary mortgage payment and the permanent mortgage payment.

2/28 Adjustable-Rate Mortgage

This is a type of an adjustable mortgage wherein it provides a two-year fixed interest rate period, then such rate shall begin to float on the basis of an index plus a margin. The fully indexed interest rate is composed of the index and the margin. This type of mortgage is often utilized as a short-term financing vehicle, which helps borrowers fix their credit and refinance their mortgage with better terms for the borrower.

This too is a risky mortgage, since the monthly payments of the borrower will surely increase as soon as the interest rate starts to adjust at a higher rate. Usually there is a very high chance that the fully indexed interest rate will be much higher than the initial two-year fixed interest rate. Once this rate increases the borrower will surely pay higher payments each month for such mortgage.

3-2-1- Buydown

This type of mortgage provides a borrower with three temporary-start interest rates. These rates will begin to increase until such time that a permanent rate is established. The reduction of temporary interest rates shall be charged by the lender to the borrower.

This mortgage type is a tool that helps borrowers with relatively low income but with excess cash to be eligible for a mortgage. It is also a tool often used by a builder as an incentive to a person in purchasing a home from that builder. Making payments to this type of mortgage is the same as paying for a mortgage so that the interest rates shall decrease.

It is important to note, however, that the reduction on interest rates with this type or mortgage is only temporary. The buyer must make a careful analysis of the data of his mortgage - so he may be able to determine that this type of mortgage is the best choice for him in his situation.

3/27 Adjustable-Rate Mortgage

This mortgage has a three-year fixed interest rate period, after which the interest rate begins to float based on a particular index plus a margin.

The purpose of this type of mortgage is to enable the borrower to repair his credit and refinance before the interest rate begins to change. This mortgage is typically used when dealing with subprime borrowers. It is also typically utilized as a short-term tool that helps the borrower refinance his mortgage into one with more favorable terms.

Many people with this type of mortgage fail to see that future economic instabilities may make refinancing very difficult for them. This eventually results in making higher interest payments, which are well beyond their financial capacity.

48- Hour Rule

It is a requirement that all information concerning transactions, which are announced on forward mortgage-backed securities, are told to the buyer by the seller. They have to do this in forty-eight hours before the settlement date of the purchase at 3pm.

This is required by the Securities Industry and Financial Markets Association. For instance, both the buyer and the seller agreed on July 14 as the settlement date. This requires that the seller should have informed the buyer on July 12 about all information pooled.

5-1 Hybrid Adjustable-Rate

Mortgage

This type of mortgage has an initial five-year period wherein the interest rate is fixed. Afterwards, the interest rate shall start to adjust on a yearly basis in accordance to an index with a margin. The fully indexed interest rate is limited by a cap structure. The index which affects the interest rate is variable but the margin is fixed for the lifetime of the loan.

A borrower who intends to refinance or who intends to move prior to the expiration of the fixed interest rate period prefers this kind of mortgage. But what these borrowers fail to take note is the fact that there is some risk in taking on this type of mortgage. Note that a borrower's personal finances and the general condition of the market would make it difficult for him/her to move or refinance after the five-year period.

5-6 Hybrid Adjustable-Rate

Mortgage

This type of mortgage also has a startup of five years for its interest to remain fixed. After such time, the rate begins to adjust bi-annually in accordance to an index plus a margin. The index state is subject to change, while the margin shall remain fixed for the duration of the loan. It is wise to remember that different indexes have different effects in different interest rate environments.

80-10-10 Mortgage

It is a mortgage wherein two mortgages are simultaneously originated.

The first mortgage has an eighty percent loan-to-value ratio while the second one has a ten percent loan-to-value ratio, which further mandates that the borrower shall pay a ten percent down payment.

This mortgage is more frequently referred to as a piggy-back mortgage. This mortgage is preferred by borrowed since they do not need to pay private mortgage insurance.

Energy Improvement Mortgage

This is a type of mortgage that sets aside a certain amount of money for home improvements that will increase the energy efficiency of the home.

This type of mortgage is usually available when a house is being purchased or when it is being refinanced. Borrowers will have to pay a higher rate on their mortgage, but this additional cost will even out. This is because the energy cost of the house is greatly lowered through the efficiency of the improvements done. The monthly costs of a borrower are greatly lessened with such improvements and it also makes the home more energy efficient. Homes which are energy efficient cost more to resell than its non-efficient counterparts.

Exotic Mortgage

This is a type of mortgage which offers the borrower a lower monthly payment in the first years of the mortgage. But this is a high-risk mortgage since its terms are usually very hard to understand and it requires higher payments in the future.

People who purchase expensive homes that they cannot afford usually go for this type of mortgage. These mortgages may also be refinanced to lower their monthly payments. This type of mortgage is rarely sought for because of its risks. The payment schedule of this type of mortgage causes the borrowers to owe more than they originally borrowed.

Graduated Payment Mortgage

This type of mortgage has a fixed rate wherein the payment increases little by little from a low point until it reaches its peak and stays there. Usually, the payments made will grow from seven percent to twelve percent yearly from its base until the full amount is paid.

Growth Equity Mortgage

It is a type of mortgage that has a fixed rate but the monthly payments are increasing over a period of time - in accordance with a set schedule. The interest rate remains the same throughout the life of the mortgage.

The beauty of this mortgage is that when payments begin to increase, the amount above what would be the amortizing payment is directly deducted from the remaining balance of the mortgage. Thus, the life of the mortgage is lessened and the borrower has saved on interest.

Home Equity Conversion Mortgage

This is a type of Federal Housing Administration insured reverse mortgage, which allows its borrowers to convert the equity in their homes into cash.

The amount of money the homeowner can borrow is equivalent to the appraised value of their home but subject to the age of the borrower as well. The money advanced is against the value of the home. The interest on the money borrowed shall accrue to the loan balance of the borrower but payments must not be made until the home is sold or the borrower has died.

Income Property Mortgage

This mortgage is a loan extended to an investor, allowing him/her to be able to purchase a rental property - which may be a residential or commercial one.

This mortgage is quite difficult to qualify for and it often requires a borrower to include an estimate of the rental income expected from the property. One of the goals of real estate investors is to own a rental property but reaching this goal is harder to accomplish.

This type of mortgage requires a huge down payment compared to other mortgages, since this property is expected to generate income.

Interest-Only Mortgage

This type of mortgage requires the borrower to pay only the interest from the principal amount borrowed. Thus, the payments are constant. However, this does not last indefinitely since the borrower must eventually pay the principal amount of the loan.

This type of loan is very much useful for people who purchase homes for the first time because this type of loan allows the individual to increase his/her income first. When the period for interest-only payments has expired, the borrower can choose to renew the interest only mortgage - or to pay the remainder through standard methods like entering into a normal mortgage or liquidating the property.

Ability to Repay

It is the financial capability of a person to be able to settle his/her obligation.

This particular phrase was used in the Reform and Consumer Protection Act, which explains that mortgage originators must make sure that possible borrowers have the financial capacity to settle the obligation they are about to incur.

These originators, or simply called lenders, must look into the totality of such potential borrower's income and his existing obligations. Simply put, every lender has the responsibility of taking the necessary steps to determine the solvency and liquidity of the person borrowing from them. This is to establish that such borrower is capable of paying off all his/her obligations.

This requirement is a safety precaution for all types of lenders since they are able to determine if their money will indeed come back to them with additional interest.

Absentee Landlord

An absentee landlord refers to either a person or a juridical entity that allows other parties to lease or rent his/her/its real estate - without actually residing on the premises of that rented out property. This type of landlord can be an individual or a partnership - or even a company who has real estate holdings.

The aim of this landlord is to make money from the rental operations. Absentee Landlords with multiple real estate properties, which would sum up to a substantial investment, generally hire management companies to collect rent and look after all their properties. This type of landlord has a long-term perspective when it comes to these properties, since the amount of rental collected is quite a sizable amount that could even be a source for it to acquire more properties.

Absentee Owner

This term refers to an individual who is the owner of a particular real estate - but this individual does not reside in that property. An absentee owner does not just refer to a person but it also refers to a corporation or even a real estate Investment Trust. A single person may possess a condominium, house, or an apartment. On the other hand, a corporation can own multiple condominiums, apartment buildings or even entire shopping malls. Absentee owners intend to keep these properties in their possession so that they are able to generate a quantifiable amount of return from their investment through rentals and even capital appreciation.

The proportion of absentee owners tends to be higher when the economy and the property market are strong and the interest rates are low. On the other hand, the number of absentee owners is quite limited when the market and the economy are at a low point and the interest rates are through the roof.

Absolute Auction

This is a type of auction where the sale is given to the person with the highest bid. A good example of this type of auction would be foreclosed properties held for auction, where the winning bidder owns the property foreclosed. This type of auction happens at different venues like the online marketplace or the foreclosure marketplace - or even the live auction events. This type of auction is chosen and conducted where there is an immediate need to sell a particular item, whether it is a personal property or a real property.

Absolute Title

This title is also known as a perfect title. It allows the owner to exercise unequivocal right of ownership over the property if it is free from any encumbrance or deficiency.

This title has no attachments, liens or judgments against it. It is wise to do a title search so that you are able to determine if a certain property has an absolute title or it is one with encumbrances. This is so that you are knowledgeable about what kind of property you are about to acquire.

Absorption Rate

It is the rate in which available homes are being sold in a particular real estate market during a certain period. You are able to compute this rate by dividing the total number of available homes by the average number of sales in a month.

The significance of this rate is that it tells you how many months it takes to fully exhaust the supply of homes that there are in the market. A high absorption rate indicates that a homeowner can easily sell his/her property, since the supply of available homes in the market will rapidly shrink.

For instance, a certain city has a thousand homes that are on the market and a hundred homes are bought every month. By using the formula for this rate, we can determine that it will take ten months for all the houses to be bought.

This rate is very useful for people who want to sell their properties, since it tells them the odds of selling. Builders also utilize this rate because it indicates when it is time for them to build more homes to sell.

Abstract Title

Different from the Absolute Title, this refers to the background of a particular title. It lists down all the legal actions a particular title has been through and all those which are pending.

This is a method used to determine whether there are claims on a property. The abstract title contains all transfers, grants, conveyances, liens and encumbrances on the property. Every buyer must have this so that he/she can determine if the property is worth buying.

ABX Index

This index is commonly referred to as Asset-Backed Securities Index. It is a financial benchmark, which enables an investor to measure the total value of mortgages which are made to borrowers with weak credit.

This index is often utilized to determine whether the market for these securities is improving - or if they are worsening. If this index is increasing, this means that there is less risk with subprime mortgages.

Subprime mortgages are those mortgages which are given to people with weak credit. Thus, the ABX index is also helpful for investors who are very much interested in subprime mortgages. This index was created by Markit.

Accelerated Amortization

This enables a person with a loan to make additional payments to their bill - so that they are able to pay off their mortgage before its settlement date.

The benefit of doing this is that the total interest payments are reduced. These are actually extra payments given by the borrower with the end goal of paying down a mortgage principal sooner. When a person pays his mortgage in an accelerated manner, it has the result of decreasing the loan premium faster. It also diminishes the amount of the interest the borrower is required to pay, with the added bonus of settling the obligation in a shorter period of time.

For instance, let's say you take out a mortgage worth 200,000USD with an interest rate of 7% and it would last for 30 years. The monthly payment you are required to make is 1330.60 USD. Once you increase your payments by 100 USD per month, you are able to pay your mortgage within 24 years instead of the original 30 years. You save on interest payment for six years.

Acceleration Clause

This is a certain provision in a contract. It allows a lender to demand fulfillment of the entire obligation, or the outstanding part of that obligation, from the borrower once such borrower has violated a certain requirement.

This clause stipulates the circumstances that the lender may demand immediate fulfillment of the obligation due to him/her. This is sometimes called the acceleration covenant.

For instance, a borrower fails to make his monthly payment for a certain period of time - and such failure is one of the instances where the lender can demand the complete fulfillment of the obligation. The borrower is not only liable to fulfill the obligation at once, but also for breach of contract. This clause is therefore like a penalty imposed upon borrowers who do not honor their obligations.

Acquisition Fee

This is a fee which is usually charged by a lessor so that the expenses of arranging a lease will be covered. This fee includes charges and commissions paid for acquiring the property - like closing costs, development or construction costs, or real estate commission.

The acquisition fee may be paid at once by the buyer or the lessee or it may also be added to the loan and paid over a period of time just as long as the period of the loan.

This fee is sometimes hidden in the purchase price or the lease price. The buyer must look out for this fee. It is wise to remember that an investor must be given a breakdown of the acquisition price and an explanation of the items comprising such a price.

Acquittance

It is a document which states that a certain debtor has been released from an obligation. It is a document which ensures the lender will not or cannot request any more payments from the borrower when it comes to the debt indicated in the acquittance.

This document is usually issued by banks and other lenders to borrowers upon their final payment.

This official statement is useful in determining whether a debtor has good or bad credit.

Active Tranche

An active tranche means that a tranche of a collateralized mortgage obligation is being paid principal payments, which are then passed on to its investors. A particular tranche transitions to an active one the moment it starts receiving principal payments in accordance with the schedule set in the collateralized mortgage obligation prospectus.

After the last payment is made to an active tranche, it is then retired and the next tranche is activated. This process continues until all the tranches in the collateralized mortgage obligation has been retired.

Ad Valorem Tax

The term 'ad valorem' stands for according to value. It is a tax that is based on the assessed value of the real estate property or the personal property. This tax can be imposed on property or on imported items.

Depending on where you reside, Ad Valorem Tax can be one of the major sources of income of the government. This tax is usually incurred through ownership of assets.

Balloon Loan

This is a type of loan that does not fully amortize over the period the loan runs. Since it is not fully amortized, a huge payment is required at the end of its term - so that the principal amount of the loan shall be paid plus the remaining interest. A balloon loan can be quite attractive to borrowers who intend to borrow only for a short term, since this type of loan has a lower interest rate than its long-term counterparts.

At times, this type of loan carries with it a reset option that entitles the borrower to have the interest rate reset after a certain period of time. Afterwards, a recalculation of the amortization schedule is done. For those loans which do not have the reset feature, borrowers would typically sell the property subject of the loan or refinance the loan before its term ends.

Blanket Mortgage

This type of mortgage covers multiple real estate properties. Although the properties are held as the collateral on the mortgage, each property could be sold without retiring the entire mortgage. Developers usually utilize this type of mortgage so that he/she would not need to take out multiple mortgages of so many properties. Also, a big piece of real estate can be covered by a mortgage - and such property can be subdivided and sold one by one without retiring the entire mortgage.

Capital Gain

This gain is an increase in the value of the real estate wherein the property has a higher value compared to its purchase price. This gain can only be realized when the property is sold.

Capital Loss

This loss is incurred when the price at the time the property is sold is far less that the price of the property when it was purchased.

Cash Equity

It is the amount invested by an owner in the property.

Chain of Title

A chain of title is the official record for the ownership of a property. This states the historical title transfers of that property, from the present owner to its first owner.

This is usually maintained by a centralized system and most of the time this is researched by a title company for a buyer.

Closed end Credit

A closed end credit is a loan, or an extension of a loan, where the proceeds of such loan is given in full once the loan is closed. Then, it must be paid on a specific date - including interest and finance charges.

This type of loan may require periodic payments comprising the interest and the principal, or it may require a lump sum payment at a certain date. This type of loan mandates that the borrower pays the full amount of the loan at a set period.

Co-Tenancy Clause

This clause can be commonly seen in retail lease contracts. The co-tenancy clause states that a certain tenant shall be allowed to ask for a reduced rate on his/her rent when key tenants or a certain number of tenants vacate the retail property.

A key tenant is someone who attracts people into the retail property even when the other tenants would fail to make enough sales. This is a clause that protects tenants so that they are compensated for the loss of possible buyers.

The co-tenants referred to here are the anchor tenants in a mall. These anchors are the popular stores that attract human traffic that spills over to the other not-so-popular stores in the mall. Although when the economy is not doing so well, this clause causes the loss of landlords to increase and may eventually cause them to declare bankruptcy.

Debt Buyer

Debt buyers are companies that purchase debts from creditors - but at a discounted price. They are usually collection agencies or private debt collection firms. These debts are usually delinquent and are charged-off at a fraction of their value.

Defeasance Clause

It is a clause in a mortgage that states that once the borrower has met all the mortgage terms then the title to the property shall be given to him. This clause is made as a substitute for collateral on the mortgage.

Earnest Money

It is a sum of money paid as a deposit to a seller to show that the buyer transacts with him in good faith. Usually, earnest money gives the buyer more time to look for financing. This amount of money is usually put in a trust or escrow account jointly by the buyer and the seller. This deposit shows the seller that the buyer is serious in purchasing the property being sold.

Chapter 8: Things you should know before become Landlord

If you check out the stories that are told in real estate circles, you can notice that the term "landlord" is often repeated. A landlord is the person who owns a house, apartment, land or real estate which is rented to an individual called a tenant, a lessee or renter. The tenant can be some company or business too. Instead of the landlord, you can use terms landlady (for female owners) or lessor (for both genders).

The concept of the "landlord" encourages of the Roman Empire and the manorial system, which began under it. Back then, the peasants were bound between the land and dependent on their landlords for protection and justice. These relations became widespread under feudalism.

Do you want to own a nice property? Perhaps income-producing properties like family homes, duplexes or even a smaller apartment building that are rented out to a tenant and from which you can earn a monthly stream of cash. All you have to do is to pay for the nice property and rent it. Right? It is anything but that easy, trust me.

Before you contact your real estate agent, I advise you to consider what's really important. In order to let you move forward with buying and managing a rental property, I must share some super important facts which will help you become an awesome landlord:

Initial Investment

Most of the landowners think they should pay for the purchase of the property and that's it - all investments are completed. Do not expect to start-up costs end there and be ready for additional investments.

Many countries have strict requirements for rental properties that must be met before you start renting. So, if you buy an old and damaged house, you must spend a significant amount of money to make it "rentable." You can spend thousands of dollars to repair problematic pipes and bad installation or if the foundation of the house is somehow damaged. Even if you buy a property in good condition, you may still have to make changes to match the standards.

Constant Repair Costs

If you thought you are finished investing money in your property, you are sorely mistaken. After the renovation of your house or apartment, you do not need to worry about the costs for a while and after that time usually begins a war with repairs. If you want to be a landlord, you need to be sure that you can pay for repairs. The law obliges you to do serious repairs as soon as possible and they often cost a lot. For example, if you get a call from your tenant at 1:00 am at night and he tells you the pipe in the bathroom is broken and water leaks through all house. In this situation, he expects from you to immediately call an emergency repairman to shut off the water and dry out the house. It's after hours so repairman will charge you $100 per hour. You also need to repair a leaking pipe so you will pay for delivery and installation, as well as throwing away your old, broken pipe.

Besides the costs mentioned above, you probably would need to invest some of your free time too. Some tenants will call you for lot sorts of things like changing light bulbs or repairing light switches and stuff like that.

Collect Rent

As you know, there are different types of tenants. They can be great people who pay the rent on time every month. It can also happen that you have tenants who do not always pay on time, but always let you know when to expect the rent. You are lucky if your tenants are like that because there are lots of people who don't pay the rent and don't call either. That's why sometimes you have to act like a debt collector.

You need to be able to confront your tenants. So, you have to think about that before you start renting. As a landlord, you'll have to make tough decisions. For example, you have a tenant for a few months and one month he doesn't pay the rent. You think that it's fine to wait a few days for him to call you, but you didn't hear from him for a week. Finally, you decide to call and he tells you he won't be able to pay for another 10 days. This is a situation where you have to make a choice to either let the tenant slide or to start the eviction process. If you want to be a landlord, you have to be comfortable making this kind of decision and sticking to it.

You can avoid all of that if you don't rent to anyone before checking credit history and other relevant data. You can choose among prospective tenants, but it's very important to make your decisions based on legitimate business criteria. And one more friendly advice, never make choices about tenants based on personal reasons. Don't rent your house or apartment to someone just because he is decent, likable or recommended by your acquaintance or co-worker. If potential tenant's income is insufficient to pay the rent, that makes him a bad risk for your business. Use a written rental application to properly screen your tenants to avoid problems in the future.

Cope with Problematic Tenants

Some landlords have luck with their tenants. They regularly pay the rent, treat the property as their own and don't have disagreements with neighbors. Not all people are the same, so as a property manager, you can come across with very problematic tenants. Here is what happened to one friend of mine. He agreed to rent his property to two college students. The first two months they are regularly paying rent. Then one day one neighbor called him to complain about students who play loud music late at night. He called them and no one answered the phone. Then he decided to go to the house and talk with them and he asked me to go with him. When one tenant opened the door, we were shocked by the scene that we found. The tenants had installed a fireman's pole in the center of the house, so now we have a hole in the first-floor ceiling and mess from waste concrete on the floor. They promised to pay for repair the damage they caused. As you can guess, they didn't do it.

Further developments you could only see in the movies. My friend filed for an eviction. After the hearing, they said they were sorry for what they have done and went back to the house and removed their stuff before the sheriff and we got there. When we went inside, my friend almost fainted. The house looked really terrible. There was graffiti on the walls, concrete in the toilets and sinks, stains on the floors...and the big hole in the ceiling.

If you want to be a landlord you have to have in mind that tenants can damage your investment, and not pay for repairing it. You need to master the eviction laws, and be able to use them whenever you need. That means it would be good for you to use a written lease or month-to-month rental agreement so you can document the important facts of your relationship with your tenants. It's always best to have all in written.

Managing Your Finances

If you want to become a successful landlord you have to look at property management as a rotating door. Tenants come, stay a while and go to next house or apartment. After that happens, your property may stay empty for next few months. A good landlord knows how to manage his finances during such a dry season. It is very important to know how to save and not spend money during such a period when you don't have the regular inflow of money from the rent so you can survive. One thing is sure, the finances of a landlord are not constant, so he has to go with the flow and have plans for the unexpected situations.

Always Keep Your Property Safe

People get injured all the time and that can happen to a tenant on your property. There is good chance that someone will sue you because of that. You probably have homeowner's insurance and that is great, but you still need to keep your house or apartment properly maintained to avoid possible problems of that kind. If you don't keep your property in good repair, that isn't fair if your tenants are good, and tenants may gain the right to withhold rent or move out without the need to give any notice. The good landlord has to know safety codes in the area, keep a regular maintenance and periodically check on his property. This is the only way he can sleep peacefully at night.

Provide Secure Premises

In some cities, city government has blamed landlords of houses or apartment buildings for crime in the neighborhood. Punishment for such property managers may be revoked rental licenses if city inspectors identify a certain number of criminal incidents associated with properties. So, don't let your property and people living in it to be easy marks for a criminal. Security of people's home is a very serious thing and you should take reasonable steps to protect it. They are not that expensive; you just need to get proper lights and make sure to have trimmed landscaping.

Resolve Disputes

As I mentioned before, you probably will have a conflict with a tenant over all kinds of stuff- rent, deposits, repairs, your access to the rental property, noise or some other issue which does not require an immediate warrant an eviction. In case that happens to you, it's always better to try to resolve that problem informally. If that doesn't work, ask for help from a neutral third party-consider mediation (it's often available for free or little cost from a publicly funded program). Resolve disputes with your tenants are always better without lawyers and lawsuits.

If all attempts to reach agreement with your tenant fails and your dispute involves money, the best way to deal with it is to try small claims court (you can represent yourself). Small claims court is the best choice if you want to collect unpaid rent or seek money for property damage after a tenant moved out.

Pay Taxes

It's important that you take paying taxes very seriously. Renting a property is like every other business so you have to report your income and regularly pay taxes at the end of the year. You have to be aware that you need to pay double the amount you were paying before you purchased the property for rent. You need to be able to pay taxes if you want to be a successful landlord.

Here is one trick you can do so taxes can work in your favor- if you want to sell your home but can't recoup what you invested in it. If you sell that house or apartment as your primary home, you can't claim the loss on your taxes. You have to turn it to rental property and then you can claim the loss as a business loss against any rental income received. This trick can help to reduce your tax bill so if you have a high income and claim a large loss you can save thousands of dollars.

Hire a Lawyer

There are some situations in which property owners should ask for lawyer's help. If you want to be a successful landlord, you have to be able to recognize those situations. Like any other type of business owner, you have to have a goal to make your business profitable while steering clear of liability. So, it's a smart move to hire or consult with a lawyer in order to achieve these goals. Here are some of the most situations in which you may need review or help from the attorney.

1. Evicting a Tenant

If you are interested in renting properties, you are probably hearing that in most countries a lawsuit about eviction resolves much faster than regular civil cases. So, if you are a landlord and want to be treated with such expedition, you need to follow some highly detailed rules- from notifying the tenant of the lawsuit to filing the right papers and forms. Usually, you can manage to evict a tenant yourselves, but it's better to hire a professional if:

-It is your first eviction.

-The tenant has hired a lawyer to fight the eviction.

-The tenant is an employee hired by you.

-The tenant is declared bankrupt.

2. Being Investigated or Sued for

Illegal Discrimination

It is obvious that you don't need a lawyer every time tenant accuses you of illegal discrimination. But if a prospect or the tenant sues you for discrimination and HUD or a fair housing agency agrees to investigate a claim, you'll probably have to consult a lawyer.

If you are the first-time offender, HUD administrative law judges can award a civil penalty of $16,000 you must pay + actual damages, attorneys' fees, and other reliefs. Besides that, if you become the subject of a discrimination investigation or lawsuit, it can make it to the press and harm your business' reputation. A good lawyer knows how to end the investigation or lawsuit as soon as possible and help you resolve the dispute.

3. Sued for Injury or Illness

If a tenant or other person (for example tenant's guest) claim that he/she has got injured in your possession or got sick because you were careless and threatens you with a lawsuit, hiring a lawyer is a smart thing to do. Cases of personal injury are high stakes, and a lawyer (professionals specifically in that field) knows what to do in such cases. In addition, it is very difficult to cope with the situation when a tenant suffers a serious loss. It could be very hard for you even if you are not responsible for any of that.

Any lawyer you hire will be objective when it comes to emotions detached in the case like that. He would have to be experienced in these types of situations and know how to effectively negotiate in your best interest. In case you did not know, you have right to all help you need from the insurance company but only if regularly pay them. It is their responsibility to provide you with a professional attorney to defend your rights in court.

4. Sued for Major Property Damage

You also can have problems with lodgers (tenants) or his/her guests when they think that your bad maintains of rental property caused damage to things they own. When something like this happens, it is obvious that you can expect a lawsuit. Therefore, if the tenant believes that you don't care about the maintenance of your property and that caused damage to his furniture (for example), it is certain that they will seek compensation from you.

In cases like one mentioned above, your liability policy is a very important thing. As a good landlord, you need to have ability to estimate the seriousness of the situation. When you are dealing with a high claim, it's a smart move to call your insurance company, refer the matter to them and demand the help of an attorney. The company is obligated to provide a lawyer for their users. Therefore, does not always have to be like that. There are cases when a claim is low, so you don't need to hire a lawyer because you can handle it yourself, but it does not hurt to consult with an expert from the field.

5. Audited by the IRS or Tax Agency

In case that you know that your state tax agency or the IRS will revise your return, don't panic because you may don't need to hire a lawyer. You don't have to hire any tax professional for audits in which "problematic" taxes are low (less than a few thousand dollars) and not enough to cover the expense of an attorney. Therefore, if there is a lot more money at stake you just need to contact a lawyer to help.

There are situations in which is better to be safe than sorry, so if you know that you have made a huge mistake which is still unnoticed by government, I advise you to contact your lawyer to help avoid possible serious situation, which can be very bad for you.

6. Defending Your Reputation

You probably know what negative publicity can do to your business. So, you have to be careful and wise if an accident or serious crime happen in your rented house or apartment. Therefore, you know that this is not your fault, but other people don't think that way, you have to know how to handle the press. I suppose you are not an expert in public relations so it would be wise to hire lawyer to speak for you or just to advise you what to say or do in order of drawing positive attention to your business.

7. Changing Your Business Structure

Let's say you are running the S-corporation for a few years and then decide that it would be better for your business to become a limited liability company. You can also come to an idea to become a partner with your brother, friend or colleague after years of working solo. In both cases, it's wise for you to contact your attorney and ask for advice. He can explain to you which documents you have to file depending on the type of business structure you choose. Every decision you make regarding changes we mentioned before will have important tax and legal consequences, so it's important to contact your attorney and ask help from him.

8. Purchase or Sell Your Property

You probably think that the buying and selling of possessions is one of the common things and not very complicated process. Things are not so simple, it is very complex and filled with legal risks than many people are not aware of, especially if you are a landlord and want to buy a building full of people which live in rented apartments. In that case, the advice of a lawyer can be precious because he can help you through the whole process (step by step) from negotiation to closing the deal. For example, you want to purchase a property with environmental or structural issues which came to light in an inspection report. A good lawyer can help you and commit the seller to remove liens, mortgages and tax levies to ensure you get "clean title" -it's the only way for you to have ownership that's free of claims.

Hire a Property Management Company

If you are a small landlord and own few properties you can do all work by yourself and maybe hire one employee to help you with property management. Therefore, as your incomes are increasing you will decide to buy more and more properties to rent. Then you will need more help and hiring a property management company is not such a bad idea at this point. They can be a valuable assistance to you but are not cheap at all. Let's see what property management company can do for you: advertise your rentals, collect rent, handle maintenance, and repairs, respond to complaints, pursuing evictions...

If you hire a good management company which has experience in this business, you can sleep peacefully at night because your investment is in good and competent hands. The company even can employ their own property managers if don't want to be an employer. All of that sounds really nice but can be very expensive, so you need to estimate whether such expenses are justified. The decision is yours and I can only help you by drawing your attention to situations in which you have to consider the possibility of hiring a property management company:

-When you have more than few properties or rental units.

-If you don't live nearby rental property.

-If you're not interested in property management.

-When you don't have time for property management.

-When you can pay for it.

-If you don't want to deal with employees.

If you realize that you need to hire a property management company and can afford it, be careful who you trust so you need to be wise when selecting one. I advise you to ask your colleagues for recommendations or consult the local apartment association. If you have read this chapter, you could come to the conclusion that you can make decent money by renting your properties, but you have to be a serious and responsible landlord. An investment like this you have to take only when you have financial independence at a high level. Buying rental properties can be a great opportunity to earn additional income, or even make it your primary one.

Chapter 9: Important things to know: Capital Gains

In simple words, Capital gains on investments is the difference between the sales price and the purchase price. When it comes to increasing the value of capital assets (investment or property) which now has greater value than the purchase price is called Capital gains. The gain cannot be realized until the asset is sold. The capital gain can be:

-Short-term (one year or less)

- Long-term (over one year)

A formula for calculation of capital gains may be explained like this: Capital gains = sales price of investment - (original purchase price + the cost of capital improvements) + depreciation you have previously claimed on the property.

It's important to mention that capital gains could be taxed - 25percent as short-term rate or 15 percent for investments held one year or longer. That is good news for rental property owners because they are usually held more than one year and it is subject to the reduced capital gains rate.

Capital gains rates are the same for small-scale and large-scale investment properties. This means that, whether your profit on investment property sales is $40,000 or $400,000, your federal tax rate is 15 percent. They are also applicable to other investments such as stocks. Capital gains rates can also work along with other tax benefits such as depreciation, which is a type of tax subtraction available to rental properties, and the tax-free 1031 exchange too.

Chapter 10: How House Flipping Works

If you just entered into the world of real estate and want to become a real estate agent, you better start learning about renovation. Your goal is to buy your first house, flip it, and make lots of money from it.

Now you are probably asking yourself is flipping houses such easy as it looks when you read in the previous paragraph. House flippers can make large profits on a sale, but can lose money too. You need to find a cheap home on sale. Put some money into a renovation, and then resell the house for much more money compared with the price at which you bought it. House flipping can make you enormous profits on a sale, it's fun but you must expect hard work. It can be risky if you don't know what you're doing. It's very important for you to remember that house flipping is a two-blade sword, you can make a lot of money, but you can also lose everything you own if you make a bad decision and there are a lot of decisions you have to make:

Where to Buy Property?

If you want to earn a nice amount of money, you can buy some house in an up-and-coming neighborhood and hope that new and "fancy" neighborhood will increase its value. This way you can attract buyers who are willing to pay more for luxury features and space offered in the suburbs. If all goes well, you will make serious money. But if something goes wrong - lack of funds for completion of the renovation, problems with timing, increased rate of crime in the neighborhood - you could be stuck with a house you can't get rid of.

The real-estate market is unpredictable. During a good season, you can have the upper hand and almost name the price of your house in some areas. But during a slow period, yours fixed-up homes can "collecting cobwebs" on the market for months.

What Kind of Property Do You Want to Buy?

Once you know where you want to buy, the next logical step is to decide what type of property you want to purchase. If you go for a fixer-upper, you will have to commit to improving the house, and that takes lots of time and money. If you decide to purchase a foreclosed property in an auction or from a bank, you could get it for the low price, but remember that if the previous owners couldn't pay the mortgage, they probably don't have money for maintenance, either - so you can expect bad installation, leaky roof and be ready to fight with rodent infestation.

It's almost impossible to flip a house without doing any work on it. There is a small chance to buy a new construction house, hold on to it for a few months, then sell it and make a good profit. So, you have to be willing and able to work hard to make things turn out exactly as you wanted and to accept the risk for unexpected problems in the neighborhood of your house.

Don't Over-Renovate

The next very important rule is to never over-improve a property. I advise you to first take a good research about similar properties in the area you pick. Next step is to establish the real market value of the house you want to flip, and then plan how to renovate the property to look decent. I am telling you this because you will have big trouble selling a $450,000 property in an area where the best houses are selling for $300,000.

Let's say you have a property in a desirable area that was attractive to first-time buyers. That's great! You should invest just enough to make the house attractive and functional, and leave some work to the buyers so they can upgrade and renovate in a way they like. You should buy new carpet, paint the walls and install new cover plates for switches, and have the plumbing and electrical installation tested and repaired. This house you can sell to a young family that is looking to buy their first home. They will be excited to move into a refreshed affordable house and opportunity of making upgrades as they like.

In this chapter, we took the time to write down for you the conclusions from the people who are working in real estate for years. Now you know the basics and can start with your fight for your place in the world of real estate.

Conclusion

Don't let fear dissuade you from real estate investing. Instead, learn all you can about the niche you want to get into and up your marketing game. This way, you will become a success story as far as real estate investing goes.

As beginners, it is important to know the fundamentals of real estate before going out into the field. There's a lot more to the business of real estate than just putting up vacant properties and houses for sale or rent. There are investment policies and mortgages to learn, and common mistakes you need to avoid. On top of that, you may have to exercise your communication skills to understand and communicate better with other people – clients, investors, and customers.

From the author

Thank you for purchasing this book.

I really enjoyed writing it, and I've already had some great feedback from readers who enjoyed the book. I hope you too enjoyed it.

I appreciate that you chose to buy and read my book over some of the others out there. Thank you for putting your confidence in me to help you. If you enjoyed the book and you have a couple of spare minutes now, it would really help me out if you would like to leave me a review (even if it's short) on Amazon. All these reviews really help me spread the world about my books and encourage me to write more books!

Sincerely Yours,

Carniel Moorblade

CPSIA information can be obtained
at www.ICGtesting.com
Printed in the USA
LVHW050930300621
691544LV00014B/691